RISING SUN

The Second Dawning
Soul Consciousness

CYNTHIA SANDRIDGE

BALBOA
PRESS

A DIVISION OF HAY HOUSE

Balboa Press books may be ordered through booksellers or by contacting:

Balboa Press
A Division of Hay House
1663 Liberty Drive
Bloomington, IN 47403
www.balboapress.com
1 (877) 407-4847

Because of the dynamic nature of the Internet, any web addresses or links contained in this book may have changed since publication and may no longer be valid. The views expressed in this work are solely those of the author and do not necessarily reflect the views of the publisher, and the publisher hereby disclaims any responsibility for them.

The author of this book does not dispense medical advice or prescribe the use of any technique as a form of treatment for physical, emotional, or medical problems without the advice of a physician, either directly or indirectly. The intent of the author is only to offer information of a general nature to help you in your quest for emotional and spiritual well-being. In the event you use any of the information in this book for yourself, which is your constitutional right, the author and the publisher assume no responsibility for your actions.

Any people depicted in stock imagery provided by Thinkstock are models, and such images are being used for illustrative purposes only. Certain stock imagery © Thinkstock.

Print information available on the last page.

ISBN: 978-1-5043-8052-2 (sc)
ISBN: 978-1-5043-8053-9 (hc)
ISBN: 978-1-5043-8078-2 (e)

Library of Congress Control Number: 2017907597

Balboa Press rev. date: 06/24/2017

Rising Sun

With the dawning of the rising sun, soul consciousness rises. Arousing from a discordant dream of separation, shadowy misconceptions of ego identification give way to light. Transmitted deep from within its core, the fiery strength of love's radiance sets illusions on fire. Unconditioned truth stands at the door of soul awareness, resonating higher part of being. Intrinsic song of power, oneness and wisdom illuminates pureness. Arising soul reveals the essence of its reality.

CONTENTS

Section One
Rooted In Infinite Light

Section Two
Releasing Your Inner Light

Section Three
Living In the Light of Consciousness

DEDICATION

Devoted to
Encouraging spiritual alignment;
Awakened heart opens upward channel to attune
to the authentic light of divinity within.

FOREWORD

Bound by no frontier, we journey deep within a timeless ocean, into a stardust dream of separation. Renewed by an unconditioned element of the rising sun, we arise from illusory experience to embrace the Love of Divine Soul.

INTRODUCTION

Are you ready to awaken your deepest divine potential? If you are ready to know the wealth of invincible greatness within you, then *Rising Sun* is for you. An invitation to generate an infinity of trust within your unique expression, *Rising Sun*'s "turn to any page" life-affirming poetic introspections lighten quantifiable externalities associated with day-to-day living. The intention of the poems is to make a conscious connection with the powerful silent witness within, to rise above and transform separation identification. Written simply in a variety of ways, these poems are a valuable catalyst for flourishing inner awareness. A nourished mind sanctions the inner eyes to open and thrive in certainty, assuring the unmodified light of inner recognition shines through to awaken your truth of being. Once your excellence is recognized, old behavioral patterns make room for tranquil spaciousness, allowing you to arouse alignment with the absoluteness of who you are. As the wonder of inner bliss resonates a sacred frequency, refined vibrations of iridescent awareness permeates from your true nature, shining with intuitive intelligibility. Inner life affirmations aimed at balancing resilient energy creates progressive mindsight, to align with the exquisite stillness within the awareness of the present moment. Living in the serenity of present moment awareness stimulates an untaught perception going beyond body, mind identification, to access the valiant super-power within you.

The amazing reality in attentiveness empowers self-responsibility for one's thoughts and actions revealing a continuous flowing of immeasurable synchronization. To be conscious of harmonic organization is to identify with the underlying truth supporting life in its pure, inspired essence. In the calm of love's serenity, a benevolent knowing resolves conditionality, healing the pain and fear of outward living. Present in exceled truth, with balance restored, the silent witness rises to the forefront, opposition and setbacks melt away. Inner life affirmations communicate freedom, strength, and peace, to encourage the majestic light of soul consciousness to shine through. The amount of time devoted to a practice of understanding the absoluteness of divine presence determines the quantity and quality of personal growth.

In Section One, *Rising Sun,* explores inner stillness to inspire successive levels of calm, quieting the mind of conditioning for self-inquiry. In a profound and touching way, Section Two, emphasizes emptying the mind of conditioning to recognize the abundant sacred garden of divine identity. Section Three, "Living In the Light of Consciousness" uses simple and effective poems as a catalysis to cultivate self-reliance of one's own inner power. Envisioning trust unshackles self-sufficiency, liberating loving self-recognition. Understanding the ephemeral nature of divine identity embodies the unchanging truth of the eternal spirit in our soul.

SECTION ONE

ROOTED IN INFINITE LIGHT

TRANSCENDING CONDITIONING THROUGH SELF-LOVE

From the backdrop of divine being to the forefront of learned behaviors, transcending constricting conditioning through self-love illuminates the unrestricted light of eternal radiance. Within the unformed core of nature's potential, the propensity of love propels the radiance of self-knowingness. Always present, within the unending spirit of consciousness, the ageless Divine Presence within everything cannot be created or destroyed. When poised in the emptiness of stillness the *inherent "I"* dawns. In stillness, one awakens to the silence within sound that provides discernment to know the Unconditioned Self always present in you. Releasing restrictive thoughts associated with generational beliefs, cultural bias and societal norms, allows the intuitive knowing of spiritual principles to resonate. Changeless and unbounded, letting go of limiting beliefs of a *physical "I"* clears the mind of its conditioning to be aware of the ability to bind with the bountiful divine light of unconditional love.

Infinite in power, the radiance of Love is the functional bond felt in self-awareness. Pure, open, free, the portal to self-love cannot be bound by physical means. From individuality to oneness with the Divine, the image of perfection concedes to the dynamism of consciousness within our soul. Emergent in responsive recognition, the harmonious energy of consciousness resides within the heart of soul as who we truly are. Forgiving limiting beliefs about ourselves requires lovingly looking within for accountability of our thoughts. The willingness to look inside is the readiness to open to the higher, loving presence within. When love's inner vision is in operation, we become more aware of our thoughts and

1

accept responsibility for the manifestation reflected in our lives from our thoughts. A clearer, innate perception from greater aptitudes of creative energy strengthens self-awareness and supports accountability for grander affairs. Breathing within the fire of heart's creation, the potency of love's light evolves from requesting prayer to *being* the prayer.

Accountability for thoughts compels the inherent inclination of divine consciousness as the ultimate power, wisdom and truth of our wholeness. Thoughts progressively broaden to shift insights from hunches and gut feelings to knowing and understanding Divine Presence's unconstrained attributes. Accepting these empowering qualities embodies an enhanced understanding of our wholeness. Making a conscious choice to release division perception encourages spiritual alignment. A spirit of introspection affirms our true nature of wholeness. Taking responsibility for thoughts reflects how detaching from a conditioned identity simplifies complex stresses and struggles to focus on making space for soul consciousness.

Rising Sun's sacred poems of healing transcends outward conditioning to stimulate soul awareness through introspection. It is incredible how focusing on the natural endowment within our soul empowers healing communication. In as little as five minutes, greater possibilities for self-recognition open in your life. These single-pointed poems are affirmations designed to nurture divine expression. Before reading a poem, find a quiet place where you will not be disturbed. Take a moment to still yourself, using the breath to connect with the peace of the inner self. Sit with your back straight and your eyes closed. Remove your attention away from the mind by observing the movement of the breath to calm the mind. As you inhale, observe how your abdomen rises and on the exhalation, it drops. In the stillness of the breath, inhale confident vitality, wholeness, and composure, allowing the buoyance of the breath to infiltrate throughout the body. Exhale through the mouth, releasing any residual stress. Continue taking serene breaths. With each breath, witness the chatter of mind slow down and the body relax a bit more to attune to the sacred wisdom of self-knowledge. A subtle, unobtrusive mind communicates an uncomplicated lightness that balances the body. While you are centering within, it is ok to allow thoughts to be. Not attaching to any one thought, when you observe your thoughts without judgement, you allow them to drift like clouds in the sky. Watch how the breath soothes the mind and the body, creating an intimate understanding of selfhood. Connect with the living presence within the body. While your awareness journeys deeper within, feel the aliveness of the body's energy field. When you center your attention on what you are feeling, your awareness within the profoundness of your unconditioned self grows stronger. Envision the luminous energy of the inner self. Abide in its dimensionless qualities as you detect an inner space of remembrance. Feel the responsive acquisition of insightful awareness and intuitive knowledge. Far more than a physical body, we are not the experience, but rather the deep-seated experiencer, of an indestructible reality. Rooted in divinity, the unconfined compassionate wisdom of truth operates across the formlessness of time and space, past limitations and change, the infinitude of the Absolute within strengthens the memory of our indivisible whole.

RISING ABOVE INDIVIDUALITY

Image of primal origin
Reservoir of evolutionary depths
Riding waves of universal collectivity
Ocean of imperceptible inclusiveness
Spiraling patterns of intuitive intelligence
Uncoil layers of extraordinary realities
Unconditioned extensiveness
Nature's wisdom pulsates insight
In the formation of creative soil
Pure foundation incarnates
Genuine peace, calm, and poise
Incubation gathers infinite power
Moving mountains of limitations
Swallowing illusion of separate self
Returning to light's truth
Intergraded beyond density

Inner Life

Unshakable inner peace
Subtle yet profound
Resiliently moving
Selflessness
Vitalizing, animating
Unbounded power
Divine footsteps
Outline limitlessness
Ancient of Days
Gracefully stirring innermost interest
Evoking certainty
Mind, body, spirit connection
Evolving eternal joy
Unifying ascent

EARTH ANGEL ANESE

Draped in an essence beyond measure
Sacred musical note
Expression of admiration
Comprehensible hope
Emblem of love's comfort
Resolute assurance
Balanced, resourceful treasure
Radiating resilience and balance
Prominent sentiments forthright
Exquisite expression of sincerity
Marvelous grace filled with dignity
Blending beauty and rhythm
Soft, warm, nurturing creativity
Virtuous life, truthful nature
Exuding wisdom with refined taste
Authentic, genuine, unconditional friend
Spreading finery and comfort
Naturally free without end
With mission fulfilled
September fifth, before daylight
On seraphic wings, Mother-Spirit took flight

RISING SUN

Inside unmolded matter
Organic silence gathers
Stillness
Sojourning across barriers of time
Eclipsed by hurdles of space
Abiding core ignites
World of untaught treasure
Rousing attainment unmeasured
Vibrating permeated light
Dawn's unbounded embrace
Awakens consciousness of soul
Inciting self-directed evolution
Lustrous framed eternal fire
Innately coated bliss
Origin upwelling
Sacred identity
Bursting forth
Flourishing
In the present moment

Primordial Reality

Secret of inborn urge
Echoes origin of truth
Love smiles
Reflecting bliss
Distance disappears
Pure inner spacelessness
Impartial, silent, still
Vision of resilient reality
Correlating true strength
Attaining birth
Recognition of self
Life energy
Boundless
Permeating time
Casting forth
Calm and stormy folds of a dream of separation
Discerning absolute identity
You, the observer
You, the character
You, as in me as in us
Combined

Soul Consciousness

Temple of incubation
Embodies truth and beauty
Ancient faceless lifeline
Blest soul
Feather of agile affection
Changeless knowing behold
Maturing self-expression taking form
Evolution of a soul
Formless, authentic, alive, breathing
Inhaling fulfillment
Conscious in direction
Un-manifest to manifest
Complete and replete
Mirror of matter's essential nature
Reveals the Unborn One

CONSCIOUS PRESENCE

Contemplating inner presence
Inborn nature knows
Nurturing innate faculties
Instinctive worthiness grows
Envisioning pure, unlimited consciousness
Self-limiting conditions abandoned
Processing thoughts of integrity
Gifts of uplifting energy flows
Detaching from false perceptions
Unchained delusions roll
Feeling inner strength mounting
Living fullness with physical ease
Quiet mind's active assurance
Transforms night into day
Sanctions understanding
Influx of insights increase
Unconditional discernment
Will to mature self-awareness
Wisdom's inner presence released

INVITATION TO OPENNESS

Spheres of mental fluidity
Attributes of creativity mold
Manifestations of integrity
Bare olden depths of gold
Influxes of uncharted self
Seen in miracle of light
Incomprehensible expression
Indivisible whole unfolds
Inseparable identity
Interrelation grows
Airs of selfishness cede
Aligned in involution
Invitation to openness
Self-love and respect beholds

Overseeing Illusion

Small hour of illusion holds
Fragmented spaces it cannot control
Supporting primordial patterns
Giving truth to misconception
Everyday complications fade
Here and now, kindness and compassion
Strengthen inward power
Multi-dimension thinker
Articulates noble heart
Subtle energies of perfection
Balanced in peace and stillness
Presence arises throughout consciousness
Natural vast grandeur
Content with implicit trust

Certainty of self-knowing
Infinite self
All abundant
Aware

Inside the Sound of Silence

Inside the sound of silence,
Secrets of divinity grow
From beginning to infinity
Nonjudgmental serenity flows
Stillness correlating purity
Exalted inner peace resounds
Calm mind communicates
Non-linear perception activates
Tranquility articulates wonders
Spiritual heart pulsates
Living power of miracles
Illusion of separation collapses and dissipates
Clear consciousness knows
Everywhere-ness exonerates
Realms of awakened knowledge
Subtle yet profound
Energy of truth
Poised within its sound

Sacred without Sin

Virtue of essence
Birthmark of nature's perfection
Still pools of mystical energy open
Present, powerful, all knowing
Fields of graduated power
Glow with unrestrained light
Air of understanding hears
Instincts channeling fact
Wealth of love proclaimed
Within the whole mind
Façade of age-old impressions
Surrendered
Enlightened expressions
Sojourn subtle levels of reality
Remembering pure state of being
Absolute authenticity
Poised in truth

Garden of Ambient Sound

Rhapsody of measure
Vibrates a self-expressive dance
Immortal soul combined with substance
Creative choice not of chance

Manifested symphonies
Profound beauty and peace
Syncopation of integrity rings
Mesmerizing garden of miracles
Spiritual counsel sing

Exotic harmonies
Golden state of mind brings
Horizons of increasing consciousness
Divinely connected gatherings
Intended for all beings

Spiritual Realm

On the shores of rousing mindfulness
Self-knowingness chose
Moment by dynamic moment
Consciousness grows
Ascending possibilities
Power of perception beholds
In the universe of spirit, mind, and matter
Time-space pilgrim
Evolving soul
In and through wonder
Immortal understanding bestowed
Passing intervals of life experiences
Insights of variability
Disclosed
Focused on exquisiteness
Messages received from spiritual guides
Divine quality
Mystical exposed

INSTINCT

Behind instinctive eyes
On laterals of astral skies
Heritage of sovereign reality dawns
On edge of underlying layer
Perched above perceptual interpretations
Vibrations of absolute origin spawn
Listening within silence
Understanding stillness
Unconditioned energy
Vitalized
Authenticity reawakens
Soul consciousness

Liberated Self

Centered in the present moment
Awareness, breathing grace
Omnipresent holistic eyes
Perceptual levels, ascending space
Meditation unravels union and oneness
Brilliant being of wisdom relates
New in every moment
Equanimity of mind, balanced emotional state
Higher intuitive realms
Divine potentials communicate
Accessible intelligence
Untold ancient and future
Meandering on horizon
Magnitude of untaught truths
Being present
Here and now, living
Self-actualizing
Shining bright

COLLECTIVE HEALING

Reality,
Birthless
Deathless
Reconciled presence
Love
Invigorates
Bracing souls
Give rise
Truth,
Give rise
Faith
Each moment's precision
Restoring perfection
A mountain of strength
Love's embrace
Tracing, arching, moving
Dropping along, free
A butterfly,
A grain,
An open sky
Emerging upon its sweeping nature
Forever indivisible, limitless, and unified

Impersonal Mind

Beyond perception
Trickling streams of consciousness glow
Intuited without thinking
Inclusive awareness of soft water's flow
Faculty of wisdom
Understanding identity flows

Discernment of unlimited strength
Interrelatedness knows
Compassionate in nature
Feeling of connection grows
Availability through every measure
Inherent being bestows

REMEMBERING YOU

Breaking night
Unshakeable insight
Intuits
Flashes of innate truth
Light of unlimited core
Presence of absolute
Revealed
Divine identity
Essence of you

INNER RECOGNITION

Answer of divine perception
Sooths rampant mind
Responsive, subtle powers
Illuminate freshness
Isles of intuition
Generate discernment
Outpouring of greatness sounds
Subliminal reality known
Organizing, moving, flowing, complete
Intention escalates
All-encompassing intelligence resonates
Consciousness awareness supplied

INTEGRITY

When outside forces seem strong,
Within the solitude of form
All answers flow
Absolute power
Grounded within chambers
Beneath threshold of consciousness
Sustaining spiritual heart
Unconditioned love and freedom
Guides, guards, protects from dis-ease.
Insight, discernment, and confidence
Rhythmic succession
Compassionate soul
Trusting intangible
Synchronicities increase
Stimulating cycles of solutions
Cascading creative truths
Selfless harmony

I Am

I am energy's fire
Experiencing heart's desire,
Exploring essence unborn
Open beyond form
Observer and observed
Life unlimited, invincible, undying
Feel me
A soulful, radiant smile
In deep, blissful joy
Delicious inspiration
Sweet conscious ecstasy
Taste me
Spiritual sensitivity
Silent promise activates
Ancient knowing
Hear me
Tree of life
Angel of twilight
I am
Journeying spiritual states
Depths of seas
Air of trees
Soil beneath your feet
Higher nature of soul

Etheric untold
Spiritual realms manifest
Touch me
Inside, limitless freedom
Outside, dimensions ahead
Unaware of my perfection
Together as one
Know me
I am truth
I am light
I am love
Consume me
Eternity of day
Master me

ETHERIC PLANE

Absent from a world abandoned
Acquiring higher spheres
Direction
Secure in heart
Wisdom's glow
Consulting warmth of soul
Faith penetrating matter
Reshaping from within
Recognizing divine intelligence
For that reason, it is essential to trust
Accurate within the heart
Essence's unification
Peaceful inner awakening
Consciousness of all
Honoring spirit's call
Nurturing the power within
Etheric
Involution

LIVING FROM WITHIN

Alive
Feeling momentum
Soul thriving
Transcendental impressions
Unconfined
From nonphysical realms to next
Silent progression at best
Discernment blooming
Imminent increase
Within reach
Greater knowledge unfolding

SECTION TWO

RELEASING YOUR INNER LIGHT

ROOTED IN PRESENCE

Centering in the light of present moment awareness involves doing away with external distractions of living in the past or waiting for future projections. An effective strategy for being aware of what is right here, right now, in this moment, is breath perception. Gently close your eyes and take a few moments to develop mindfulness of the breath. Feel the softness of the breath as you inhale. Visualize the breath as soothing white light flowing through the nostrils, filling the lungs, and then follow it throughout your body. Once you have established breath perception, position your attention at the top of your head. Breathe in the light, allowing it to enter through the crown of your head. Follow the light in and allow the breath to flow inward to each part of the body: your throat, shoulders, arms, torso, hips, thighs, knees, legs, ankles, down to your feet. Just let the light flow throughout the entire energy system. Notice the pause between the rise and fall of the abdomen on the inhalation and exhalation. As you follow the breath throughout the body, notice any tightness it might be holding. Meditate on allowing the breath to create a space where you observe stressed areas. Allow the lightness of the breath to dissipate any distractions. As you read the following poems, you will begin to realize feelings of inner peace and strength emerging, penetrating your body and settling into your soul.

SILENT AWAKENING

Sunrise of inner space
Place of no time
Energizing light of wholeness
Replicating immutable oneness
As well
As easy
Living morning dew
Subtly reaching within
Inspiring blooms
Spiraling brand new
Mounting strength
Movement grand
Eve of majestic possibilities
Retrieving awareness of ultimate reality
Opening to magnificent immortality

One Love Deep

Like the hidden depth of ocean water
Great self-sufficiency
Unfathomable resonant feeling
Inherent stillness
Entrenched with renewing power
Bountifully rich
Innately free
Vast enlightened being
Immersed in abundance
One love deep
Multifaceted unity

Intuitive Truths

Inherent strength of voice and heart
Luminous dimensions of trust start
Sacred consciousness
Ascends current perceptions of reality
Golden purpose
Love and sincerity
Reign within absolute totality
Pure serenity
Regenerates the soul
Intuitive truths
Felt and told

EXPANDING LIGHT

Liberation from judgment
Decreeing simplistic sight
Flashes of illumination
Reveal expanding light
Radiance's shimmering grace
Memorable healing taking place
Harmonizing vibration
Song of elation
Melodies of higher frequencies
Resonate

SELF-AWARENESS

Submerged in a body
Soul awareness sleeps
Enclosed in earthly shell
Ripples of self-realization
Expand and leap
Connection to Source
Calming mental, physical, emotional chatter
Mindful meditative state
Truly matters
More inner peace
During soulful stay
Harmony taught in a thorough, detailed way
Path to realization
Focuses on inner awareness
Soul's potential in session
Creates clarity for progression
Intuitive
Abstract awareness
Released

AWAKENING

Looking past isolation
To oneness of heart
Eternal Supreme
Ever-present, all knowing, absolute from start
Recognized perfection surrounded by frame
Connected inside present moment
Aware of fragmented misperception
Dream of separation let go
Breathing in rapport with the soul
External distractions depart
True nature building momentum
Comforting trust
Conscious living
Unity heard
Know you are already whole
One spirit in soul
As above, so below

REFLECTION OF HEAVEN

Unifying attribute complete within
Inner eye perceives infinite capacity
Accepting unbounded ability to carry out
Mortal release
To eternity

NATURE OF SOUL

Within the ease of simplicity
Beats the heart of soul
Living, loving, feeling
Flavor
Alive
Undefined and unstructured
Loving essence
Living in simplicity
Creating warmth
Understanding
Permanent haven of tranquility
Sensational treasures of veneration, wonderment, awe
Concede to reverence
Healing
Moral fiber
Discover
The thinker behind the thought
The observer of the observed
Self-awareness

INFINITE

Feeling
Ever increasing levels of consciousness tower
Illuminating unnoticed insight and power
Acknowledging
Sacred heart
Liberating mind, body, spirit
Alive within

Strengthening integrity tenfold
Emerging worthy and bold
Purifying personality's hold
Assisting fate of destiny's role
Secure embryonic soul
Identity
Infinite within

FORGIVENESS

Forgiveness is a nod to God
Protection from decay
Forgiveness is a breath of life
Permeates mind throughout the day
Sees beyond the body
Holy frame of divine array
Forgiveness understands compassion
Rejoices in serenity
Forgiveness is
Extraordinary peace
A place of union where all souls meet

MYSTICAL

A mansion world suitable for mortal climb
Unchanged bridge
Tenderly uncovers
Beautiful innermost place
Healed in silent contemplation
Loving thoughts light the way
Boundless paradise rise
Within

Rendezvous
Talking, laughing,
Enjoying the present moment
No inhibitions
Free
Silent sphere
Just being me
Spiritual maturation

Halo

Love's identity
Sings a holy song
Extended and extending
Measure of reality
Heaven's unchanging gift
Shared
Sparks of beauty
Individualized unity
In relationship with each other
In relationship with the Source
Joined in truth
Light, joy, and peace strong
Halo of life
Born of power
Dance of dawn
Fire

CONSCIOUS LIVING

Beyond external images
Standing in the light of present moment awareness
Inner wakefulness
Truth, integrity
Watchful, alert
Beyond the surface engulfed
Feeling
Golden white rising sun within
Touching life
Mindful living
Accelerates internal perception

Releasing Blockages

Consent to letting truth's blessing flow
Awaken
Quiet sensations of inner trust
A self-actualizing expression
Its effortless strength
Unstoppable assuredness
Assent to truth
Discernment and appreciation
Spontaneous wonder comply
Spiritual confidence's course
In silent expectancy
Released

STILLNESS

In the presence of stillness,
Sincerity breathes
Truth echoes free
Fountains
Emerging
Pure veracities
Authentic precision
Within the center of being
Gazing at its holiness
Love and peace reality
In the presence of stillness
Conscious rivers see
Living plains
Grow
Life flows
Perfection spoken in so many ways
Wholeness, truth, balance
Unchanged

ONE

Designed as created
Certain free
It is not by chance
I am, we are
Receiving perfect balance
Perceiving simplicity
Vitality and power
Self-sufficiency
Inherent strength of adoration
Uninhibited ecstasy
Harmonic concerto
Loving life
Honoring individuality
Liberated in primal silence
Calm of wisdom
Expanding from restrictive thinking
Thoughts of fear released from me
Opening to pure consciousness
In route to vast
Power of mindfulness

I

I am
All
In rhythm
Feeling oneness
Wholesome attitude
Nonjudgmental reality
Naturally *being*
Connected in sincerity
Designed with purpose
Dance of love reflects from me
Self-oneness with all creation

In This Perfect Moment

I am eternal peace
I know no grief
I have everything and nothing

In this perfect moment
Time is nonexistent
I experience contentment of wholeness
I am
Liberated
I am
Spiritual maturity
In this perfect moment
I live in ease, in peace

Soul

Limitless, wandering,
Dropping within
Silent missive
Driving, lifting
Gale
Exhaling sweet delight
Mild
Shifting
Earth
Peace by open poem
Beating soft against
Blurred realm
Against open ground
Against black pointed skies
Against closing calm
Dreams dissolve warm rivers
Today dizzy, like the sun in triturate

LIVING IN GRATITUDE

Thank you
Energy of health and happiness
The prosperity of your abundance
Flows my way
Thank you for surrounding me
Joyous sounds of healing's calling
Revives and reconditions
Inviting
I acknowledge your wholeness and allow
Expressions of oneness
Their right to be
Perfect blessings emerge
Soothing restoration becomes visible,
Settling into fullness
Exceptional abundance is my supply
Wellbeing miraculously materializes in my life
Excellent health is my spiritual maturation

Guardian's Watch

In mystery and majesty,
Guardians watch
Observing immortality
Wisdom of ancient
Understanding
Vastness of originality

Energizing dawn
Appears fresh and calm
Spirit of morning dew
Life blooms brand new

Intermediary for humankind
Standing grand
Reaching skyward
Calm strength
Altitude of unswerving perspective

OCEAN WAVES

Upsurges of awareness
Undulating presence
Resilient, rippling
Emergent signal
Detects an inner peace
Natural depth
Currents, gestures
Strength sways back and forth
Ripples of power
Flood awareness of perfection
Oscillations roll
Distinct depth in stillness
Potent in being
Unbiased
Flow

THE TREASURE

Touch of bountiful essence
Uncontained, forgiving, forever free
Texture of inward power makes your heart beat,
Quality of center
Reveals who you are

STILL MIND

Still mind
Worlds of inner peace
Access to soul
Self-sufficiency
Live
Wisdom of truth
Dimensions of love's unconditionality

The Voice

Think only that which you wish to experience.
Be aware of your thoughts;
They are the voice of your intentions.
Open your awareness and allow the great power of wisdom to flow.

I as All

Flame of truth in me as me
Enjoying I as all
Reflecting life's continuum
Identifying thee
I am eternal flow
Rhythm's sacred identity
Blending with indwelling divinity
Self-awareness grows

SECTION THREE

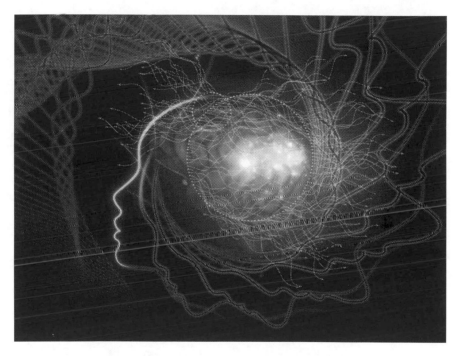

LIVING IN THE LIGHT
OF CONSCIOUSNESS

CONNECTING TO THE
SACREDNESS OF YOUR SOUL

Within the stillness of consciousness, soul's personified odyssey emerges as a unique individualized expression. As a spiritual being exploring many levels of eternal reality, the experiential journey of this life expands perceived boundaries of human consciousness. In silent spiritual union, the heart of soul regenerates the implicit trust that allows the divine flow of love to reveal its immensity. Through inner exploration, the receptivity of the presence of awareness connects the intuitive faculty to access inexhaustible oneness. Fueled with a concentrated propensity of love, soul-awareness is reborn. Articulating self-knowingness, in stillness, responsiveness opens the intuitive ears to hear understanding's exquisite voice.

Affirming the bounty within through a meditative practice increases acknowledgment as appreciation strengthens the light of divine compassion inherent in soul recognition. The evolution of soul awareness conveys a firm foundation of oneness and connectedness to loosen and free deep-rooted generational thinking habits about the self as the body; it is a matter of being conscious of the body as soul's manifestation. Accepting this ultimate perfection is operating in and through the body is accepting personal responsibility for what you create. Visualization is seeing the unseen and bringing it into manifestation. Becoming aware of your inner vastness helps you to recognize and understand the true wisdom of what "made in his image" means. As a perfect channel for understanding the abilities of self on a soul level, visualization sets self-reliance in motion. Focus your attention on the area just behind the forehead. As an evolutionary process in soul awareness, seeing through intuitive eyes of visioning, one gains passage to the innermost part of being animating the body. Within the attentive silence of your mind's eye, internal experience occurring in present moment awareness activates the spiritual power of understanding the resourceful dominion in self-love. Envisage uplifting soul consciousness is emerging. Using the breath, breathe the divine light energy of inner vision into the mind's eye, bear witness to the vital strength of your divine, creative organizing power. By focusing and envisioning self-actualization regularly, healthy equilibrium grows stronger, more permanent, and more precise.

Committing to spiritual practices of visualizations, meditation, and breath work along with the poems is an effective process you can use to provide the breakthrough to connecting to and knowing yourself as a spiritual being. Reflective and alert in the moment, still your mind with the breath, breathe quiet awareness into your body, and meditate on that unified, unconditioned self as you conceptualize with clear awareness, the spirit of your greatness unfolding into expression.

Mind is the Garden; Thought is the Seed

From the realm of great stillness and peace,
Hear the vibrant impulse of life speak
With simple acceptance and complete belief.
Acknowledge and trust your intuition.
Center and connect to your creative desires,
Dreams, inspirations,
Precision, and expectation.
Consistently reflect
Thoughts,
Truth of absolute inborn power.
After all,
Mind is the garden as thought is the seed.
Know that your thoughts today
Become your reality tomorrow in deed.

THE GUIDE

Guided by infinite wisdom,
Divine intelligence can penetrate clouds
Of want, lack, and limitation,
Revealing the light of love.
Rise above the grip of confinement;
Lift your mind.
Ignite thoughts deep within;
Feel conscious union with infinite life,
No perception of time or space.
The precision of what reality is
Unlocks the intuitive essence of love's divine flow.
Allow discernment of inner peace to open your mind.
Experience sacred understanding
Of your luminous royal self;
Touch the meaning
Of love now,
As light as a feather,
Guidance of eternal presence
Clearly heard, and all is well.

Soul Consciousness

To be human is to have a body that is the temple of divinity.
Attune your consciousness to the aliveness and wellness within it.
Animated by the spirit of self-sufficiency,
Transfer identification to identity with absolute abundance and supply.
Confidently keep your mind on the possibilities
Associated with self-sufficiency.
Sacred identification signifies the wholeness of life.
Bask in the unlimited power of self-reliance;
In doing so, attract the right circumstances to fulfill your desires.
Reveal the positive energy of strength
And independence to situations.
Acknowledge the greatness of your capabilities.
Appreciate your own instincts of inner knowing.
Experience the heightened aliveness;
Strength is found in connecting to your soul.

INNER POWER

In this moment,
Soul's soft, quiet whisper
Is here, now,
Guiding timelessness,
Voice of imagination,
Wonderment of self,
Gift of radiant life,
Virtue of purity,
Present awareness
Open at once
Eternal love.

THE DECISION

Life simply being life,
Creation from which there was none—
Mere will of the possibility that it could exist—
Therefore, it is so,
I am living.
Drawing forth from concrete earth,
I am breathing,
Drawing in;
I am growing,
Existing,
Mastering that
Single blade of grass
From which winter breaks,
My only focus.
In addition, spring arrives again.
I am first breath
From cold creation;
I am born
Bold, full of life,
The possibility within.
I exist, I am life.

THE ANSWER

Unite with the pure and simple wealth
Connected with nature's effortless
Innate flow.
Nature in its true unaltered state contains
Infinite organizing power that facilitates stability;
That equilibrium is thrown off balance
When that unified simplicity is changed.
Embrace the flow of nature's simplistic living;
Be in harmony with its uncomplicated freshness,
Magnificently.

THE WITNESS

With reverence,
Become an empowered observer of your life.
View your activities with the wisdom of noble, towering trees.
As you walk down life's path,
Step outside your aura; live as a participant and an observer.
Self-reliance is
Observing
Your actions.
Conveying organizing power,
Moreover, respect,
It also yields vibrations of value, understanding, and gratitude as well.
With the wisdom gained with reverent observation,
Self-reliant.

THE LIGHT

Glow with the unrestrained light of your inner self.
Display heartfelt confidence and immense strength,
Like that of mountains that crest a horizon.
Go within;
Open your mind.
Allow the state of solitude that connects your awareness to
The one creative cause of life
To expand.
Reserve quiet times to commune with the
powerful light of your inner self,
For this is your spiritual food and protector of your sphere.

WALKING WITH COMPASSION

Rise compassion
Open faith
Recall dreams
Shadows embraced
Sweetest of breath
Of silk
Of fine fragrance
Sound to echo
Healing arms, beyond shackles
Crash
A single raindrop booms
In the tone of God
Like a thunderstorm
Deepest on top
Like the angel's horn
One seal for spirit
The other for faith
Communion of truths
One mystical nature reflected in you

WAKING FRESH

Insight has a resourceful kind of light
Self-reliance radiates inner communication
Resourceful spectrum
Dissolves dreams
Full, awake, within
Waking fresh
One earth

REALM OF IMAGINATION

Radiating endlessly into mind's eye
Expanding inanimate imagery
Cascading oceans of energies
Embrace tangibility

LIVING IMMENSELY

Touch dimensions
Beyond space
Shapeless consciousness
Behind time
Freed of appearances
Lucid reality

GROUNDING

Unique therapeutic energy
Healing's vitality
Increase ten trillion within
Over, under, around, and through
Visualizing strength and confidence
Exuberating rejuvenating restoration
Centered from within
Harmonized and balanced
Pure energy
You

Star That You Are

Expect the highest of self in all your affairs.
Reach inwardly for that shining star that you are.
Divine principles of your inner nature
Allow
Intuitive connection,
Eternal and sacred life source,
The radiance of the God in you,
Your inherent self
Brilliantly reflecting outwardly,
Revealing the miracle of you.

THE HEART OF SOUL

Strength without form
Self-existence willed
Ever-present
Resilient and fulfilled
Timeless life
Fluidity's yield
Unconditioned love
Immeasurable
Still
Poised elasticity
Complete within itself
Transcendent, composed
Inexhaustible
Love heals

RADIANCE OF A MOMENT

Within the nonconformity of understood silence,
In the gentle wind of a calm breeze,
Harmonious ingredients of life
Increasingly I see.
Strong, a surging waterfall's spirit;
Intellectual, the wisdom of a grandiose tree;
Peaceful, a whispering brook's
Inspiring vitality;
Soothing, the effortless
Roll of an ocean;
Vastly deep, the descent of a flourishing sea.
Refreshing droplets of morning dew
Reciprocate life,
Naturally.
Phenomenal, a tropical island;
Invigorating quiver, a quake;
Powerful release, a rupturing volcano;
Emerging rhythmic rapture
Of divinity within
Awakes.
Morning sunrise,
Sacred essence
Continuous dawn of inheritance,
Melodic songs of adoration
Edify the enlightened dance
Of richly textured colors
Reflected in a glance.

Divine Droplet of Water

Divine droplet of water
Released from the ocean deep—
Its qualitativeness
Unlimited,
All-prevailingly,
Vastly deep—

Pulse of universal flow,
Ubiquitous surge
Cyclically rolling,
Absolute, pure,
Composed,
Free:
A noble course
Of mighty currents,
Bathing
In innate expression,
A mystical surging wave
Upon iridescent shore,
I sway
In the delicate scent
Of the ocean spray.
A breath of mist
Springs forth
From the shower of its rhythmic tide,
Disembarked
From flowing sea.

A coastline cove
Supplies the sense of individuality.

I am an amazing ecosystem,
Joyously glistening
In golden sunlight,
Ecstatic laughter, delight, amusing fun,
An incarnate expression
Effectively thriving,
Invincible to it all.

The ocean's motion of an ebbing wave
Distantly I heed.
Drifting echoes,
Vaporous calls drown
Within the magnitude of
My own sound.

Explosive rays of noonday sun
Assault with drying heat;
My experience begins to wither.
I grow intensively weak.
Droplets on shore
Lure together
With each receding encounter,
Listening
In silence,
Seeking relief.
Incoming tides echo;
Emerging vibrations approach,
Prismatic sounds,
Embellished tones.

A sweet scent,
Once realized,
Grows
Profound.
It is
The continuous surge
Of living water,
The source
From
Which I came.
I am
A divine droplet of water
Released from the deep sea.
From the spray
Of the mighty ocean's rhythmic flow
Comes
The pleasant-sounding roll
Of the pure, calm
Scent of living water,
Guiding me back to
The source
I am.
I am vast,
All-prevailing,
Infinite, deep.

Blossoming of the Soul

Unveiling mind
Place of no time
Centered in sacredness
Blossoming soul
Gently unfolds
Opened and released
Deep-rooted emergence
Displaying self
Complete

UNBOUND

All-encompassing light
Symphonic sight
Unbounded with dynamism
Exalted quality of sound
Unblemished perfection
Found
Creative cause of life
Wound within
Surface

Natural Living

The break of dawn
Unwaveringly crests a horizon,
Participating with observation:
Newfound resilience,
Immense strength,
Happily shining
Dignity and wisdom.

FROM THE HEART

Instrument of core energy
Soul of living
Being, in tune,
Affluent sound,
Heaven on earth ringing melody of heart,
Living etheric song
Singing animation,
Fully awake,
Residing within
Expression of spirit
Voices harmony
Aura of self-knowing unsealed
Pure image
Divinity of soul

THE EMINENCE OF YOU

In the creator's consciousness
Are you.
Subsiding in his energy
You do.
While the earth revolves,
So do you.
As the rain continues to flow,
You do too.
In the same way the seasons carry on,
You do.
The moon has phases,
Like you do.
As to how I know,
I am the same as you.
Energy wells up,
Lifecycle,
Illusion of time
It goes
It flows
It grows
To the eminence of you.

Matter of Being

Infinite light is the flow through which information travels. As it travels through productive frequencies, energies of harmonious healing filled with knowledge create ideal conditions for facilitating self-understanding, thus self-reliance. Communicated within the limitless illumination of present moment awareness is the spiritual energy field that can increase the emerging flow of information to awaken soul consciousness during this lifetime.

While in physical form, we become bound with an unbalanced sense of separation. We travel a subdued path of distraction, searching for self-understanding, creating a sluggish energy for what is experienced. We travel through life at a limited capacity, when in reality the abundance of absolute, pure love is right here, in present moment consciousness.

Present in all levels of life, living in the moment means to acknowledge everything is an aspect of the eternal God. At the level of self-consciousness, is the knowingness of being wholly aware of who you are.

Self-awareness calls for living consciously. It means living from the untaught, changeless presence within yourself. To know yourself is to operate from the stillness of present-moment oneness, to identify your*self* as an indivisible union of consciousness, allowing the soul-voice of divine reality expression. When not caught-up in outside influences or judging appearance, the mind is able to focus on the spiritual activity within the body with certainty of its essential nature to guide us to our greater good. Living from that quality of being brings about the perception that the body is a vessel that houses the essence of infinite intelligence. Awareness of inner reality unites the pieces of fragmented thinking to the divine image indwelling. Its truth eliminates the evasiveness associated with separation to emerge from partitioned elusive categories, conveying wholeness of being, oneness. When we live consciously, we know the Eternal Oneness of Being. With no beginning and no end, the present moment is who "I am."

I am my own balm, the salvation of my future. I am my children. I am my own sister. I am my brother. I am the intuitive knowingness of spiritual consciousness!

When recognized and understood, one does not validate being with material things. As a matter of being, the sense of separation has served its purpose when it no longer finds completeness in things outside of self.

The End
The Alpha
God

About the Author

Integrative health practitioner Cynthia Sandridge embraces the gentle, non-invasive, hands-on healing art of Reiki and therapeutic massage. Co-founder of Nucleus Holistic Healing, Sandridge is a member of United Nations Association of the USA, Ayurveda Health Practices, Reiki Healers Worldwide, and Light Workers of the West. She attended the Healing Arts Institute, Sacramento City College, and the University of the Pacific. Sandridge is a Certified Massage Therapist and Reiki ii Practitioner, as well as holding degrees in math, engineering, and environmental science.

AUTHOR'S NOTE

The author explores the path toward a self-directed evolution to connect readers to the absolute self. Touching the dynamic miracle of inner space to expose the organizing power of unconditioned consciousness, her message of self-awareness is simple: With unrestrained focus, find that still, quiet place to awaken the natural inclusiveness of sacred identity. Within this living reality, she encourages readers to center within its innate light and become more mindful of the higher self.

REFLECTION PAGE

REFLECTION PAGE

REFLECTION PAGE

REFLECTION PAGE

REFLECTION PAGE

REFLECTION PAGE

REFLECTION PAGE

REFLECTION PAGE

REFLECTION PAGE

REFLECTION PAGE